1·9·9·1 THE YEAR I·WAS BORN 1·9·9·1

Compiled by Sally Tagholm

Illustrated with photographs and drawings by Michael Evans

Puffin Books
in association with Signpost Books

PUFFIN BOOKS

Published by the Penguin Group
Penguin Books Ltd, 27 Wrights Lane, London W8 5TZ, England
Penguin Books USA Inc, 375 Hudson Street, New York, NY 10014, USA
Penguin Books Australia Ltd, Ringwood, Victoria, Australia
Penguin Books Canada Ltd, 10 Alcorn Avenue, Toronto, Ontario, Canada M4V 3B2
Penguin Books (NZ) Ltd, 182-190 Wairau Road, Auckland 10, New Zealand

Penguin Books Ltd, Registered Offices; Harmondsworth, Middlesex, England

Published by Penguin Books in association with Signpost Books
First published 1996
10 9 8 7 6 5 4 3 2 1

Based on an original idea by Sally Wood
Conceived, designed and produced by Signpost Books Ltd, 1996
Copyright in this format © 1996 Signpost Books Ltd,
25, Eden Drive, Headington, Oxford OX3 OAB, England

Text copyright © 1996 Sally Tagholm
Illustrations copyright © 1996 Michael Evans
Editor: Dorothy Wood
Designer: Carol Marsh

Acknowledgements: Mirror Group Newspapers Ltd. for the photographs and
Hugh Gallacher for his invaluable help in retrieving them from the files

ISBN Hardback edition 1 874785 12 0
ISBN Paperback edition 0 14 038536 3

Colour separations by Fotographics Ltd
Printed and bound in Belgium by Proost Book Production

Front cover photographs
Top: Ming Ming, Bottom: The Batmobile, Bottom Right: Paul Gascoigne

Back cover photographs
Left: Leroy Burrell, Right: Prince William

UK Fact File 1991, MCMLXXXXI

Total area of the UK	244,100 sq kms
Capital City	London (1,580 sq kms)
Population of UK	56,467,000 *Females* *29,123,000* *Males* *27,344,000*
Births	793,000
Marriages	349,739
Deaths	646,181
Most popular girl's name*	Elizabeth
Most popular boy's name*	James
Prime Minister	John Major
Head of State	Queen Elizabeth II
Poet Laureate	Edward (Ted) Hughes
Astronomer Royal	Professor Arnold Wolfendale
Royal Swan Keeper	FJ Turk
Royal Barge Master	R Crouch
Archbishop of Canterbury	*(until April)* Robert Alexander Kennedy Runcie *(from April)* Dr George Carey
Presidency of EC	*Jan-June* Luxembourg *July-Dec* The Netherlands
Members of EC	Belgium, Denmark, France, Federal Republic of Germany, Greece, Ireland, Italy, Luxembourg, The Netherlands, Portugal, Spain, The United Kingdom

John Major

The Queen

Ted Hughes

Dr George Carey

* according to The Times newspaper

Champions of 1991

World Scrabble Champion
Peter Morris, of Michigan, US

Miss Pears
Sarah Bell, of Ambleside, Cheshire

Car of the Year Renault Clio

Pipe Smoker of the Year
Sir John Harvey-Jones

World Snail Racing Champion
Streaker

BBC Sports Personality of the Year
Liz McColgan, of Scotland

Nobel Peace Prize
Aung San Suu Kyi

World Town Crier
Graham Keating, of Sydney

World Memory Champion
Dominic O'Brien

British Milkman of the Year
Nigel Matthews,
of Blythe Bridge, Staffs

Miss World Miss Venezuela
(Ninibeth Beatriz Leal Jimenez)

Miss Beautiful Eyes
Tiffany Stanford, of Birmingham

Miss Brightest Smile
Mathilda Hamer, of Eastbourne

Actor of the Year Sir Ian McKellan

Actress of the Year Kathryn Hunter

FA Cup Winners Tottenham Hotspur

World Motor Racing Champion
Ayrton Senna

World Rugby Champions Australia

Crufts Champion Raycroft Socialite

Showbusiness Personality of the Year Nigel Kennedy

Black Pudding Champion
Fred Stahly, of Kirkaldy, Fife

British Crossword Champion
Norman Maclean, of Edinburgh

❄ JANUARY ❄

Richard Branson crosses Pacific by hot air balloon

Tuesday January 1

❄ Bank Holiday.

❄ No Smacking Week is launched by the End Physical Punishment of Children Group.

❄ Goodbye to the old-style 5 pence coin, which stops being legal tender today.

Wednesday January 2

❄ The Queen announces the appointment of a new Astronomer Royal. He is Professor Arnold Wolfendale (63) of Durham University.

Thursday January 3

❄ The adder, the freshwater pearl mussel and the Allis shad (a rare type of coastal herring) all become protected species in an amendment to the 1981 Wildlife and Countryside Act.

Friday January 4

❄ A whale measuring nearly 8m is washed up on Cefn Sidan Sands at Pembrey, Dyfed, the only Welsh beach to receive the Blue Flag for bathing standards.

Saturday January 5

❄ Thirteen people die as gales sweep Ireland at 160 kph. Ferries across the Irish Sea are cancelled and the Isle of Man is cut off.

Sunday January 6

❄ The Decade of Evangelism is launched in cathedrals, churches and chapels all over Britain.

❄ Sadler's Wells Theatre, London, celebrates its 60th birthday and pays homage to its founder, Lilian Baylis.

Monday January 7

❄ Strictly no parking for more than 7 km of main road between Archway and the Angel in north London as Britain's first Red Route clearway is launched. (Fines: £16 per parking ticket or £80 for being towed away).

Tuesday January 8

❄ Six ferries are stranded in the English Channel for hours after the 1 tonne passenger ferry *Fantasia* gets jammed in Dover harbour in storm force winds.

❄ Sorley MacClean (79), who lives in Skye, becomes the first Gaelic poet to win the Queen's Gold Medal for Poetry.

Wednesday January 9

❄ Crufts Dog Show, transferred from Earl's Court in London to the NEC in Birmingham, celebrates its centenary with a record 22,993 entries.

❄ Shelley, a rare Australian Partula mirabilis snail, sets off by car from London Zoo, to join 5 potential mates at Nottingham University.

Thursday January 10

❄ Forty-six competitors take part in the first long-distance event (25km along Perth's Swan River) at the world swimming championships in Australia. Chad Hundeby, from California, USA, wins in 5hr 1min 45.78 sec. Shelley Taylor-Smith (AUS), is the fastest woman, with a time of 5hr 21 min 5.53 sec.

Friday January 11
❋ The Worcester County Cricket ground and racecourse are submerged as the river Severn burst its banks. It rises 3m above its normal level after days of torrential rain.

Saturday January 12
❋ A Clumber spaniel (2) called Raycroft Socialite (known as Garfield), from Co. Cavan, Eire, becomes Supreme Champion at Crufts Dog show in Birmingham.

Sunday January 13
❋ Rocky, a dolphin (21) from Flamingo Land in Pickering, N. Yorkshire, flies by jumbo jet from Heathrow to Venezuela on the first stage of his journey to an animal sanctuary in the Caribbean.

Monday January 14
❋ Back to work for both Houses of Parliament in Westminster after the Christmas holidays!

❋ Bristol Water lifts its drought restrictions after recent heavy rain replenishes supplies.

Tuesday January 15
❋ Richard Branson and Per Lindstrand lift off from Miyakonojo, Japan, to cross the Pacific by hot air balloon.

❋ An injured seal, found on the beach at Santander, Spain, is taken back to the Bay of Biscay on board a Brittany Ferries ship.

Wednesday January 16
❋ Operation Desert Storm: The US launches a series of air raids on Iraqi troops who continue to occupy Kuwait, despite a UN deadline.

❋ Nine Aboriginal skulls, which have been held in Edinburgh's medical school for nearly 100yrs, are flown back to the National Museum in Canberra, Australia.

Thursday January 17
❋ Richard Branson and Per Lindstrand land on frozen Lac La Martre, North Western Territories, Canada, after completing the first hot-air balloon crossing of the Pacific. They wandered thousands of kilometres off course into the Arctic.

❋ King Olav V of Norway (87), dies after a heart attack at his country home near Oslo.

Friday January 18
❋ Iceland's Mount Hekla, known as the Mountain of Hell, erupts.

❋ The Home Office issues a special warning about the disintegrating Soviet space station *Salyut 7* which is about to re-enter earth's atmosphere and will orbit England and Wales twice each day!

Saturday January 19
❋ At the Golden Globe Awards in Los Angeles, USA, Kevin Costner's film *Dances with Wolves* wins awards for best dramatic picture, best screenplay and best director.

Sunday January 20
❋ For the first time in 300yrs, Lloyd's of London is open on a Sunday to provide insurance for ships entering the Gulf War zone.

Monday January 21
❋ An electrical storm and tornado sweep through Sydney, Australia, leaving one person dead, more than 50 injured and an estimated £140 million damage.

❋ Norway's new King Harald V takes the oath of office in Oslo. Coronations are not allowed in Norway.

Tuesday January 22

✽ The Soviet Union withdraws 50 and 100 rouble notes from circulation in an attempt to control the money supply.

✽ The circumflex is saved from extinction in France by the Academie Française.

✽ Comedian Ken Dodd is named *'Jester of the Year'* by the Cartoon Club.

Wednesday January 23

✽ Aberdour, nr the Forth Bridge in Fife, Scotland, wins British Rail's *'Best Station'* title.

✽ A pair of Napoleon's dirty black silk socks is sold for £3,300 at Sotheby's, London.

Thursday January 24

✽ 260 pilot whales, stranded on a beach on New Zealand's South Island, are saved.

✽ Wildlife groups protest against plans to turn the A47 Great Yarmouth to Leicester road into a dual carriageway, threatening a Site of Special Scientific Interest where the rare fen liverwort grows.

Friday January 25

✽ Burns Night.

✽ The Crown Jewels get their annual spring clean at the Tower of London. Soft detergent, sterilized water and cotton buds are used for the first time instead of traditional jewellers' rouge and whiting.

Saturday January 26

✽ Australia Day.

✽ Tests to find out more about global warming start today in the Antarctic as underwater sound waves are sent to listening posts around the world's oceans.

Sunday January 27

✽ A huge oil slick in the Gulf threatens wildlife including Audubon's shearwater, the red-billed tropic bird, the turtle and the dolphin. Also at risk is the dugong, or sea cow, which lives on the sea grass beds along the Gulf.

Monday January 28

✽ A special survey by Cadbury reports that 500,000 tonnes of chocolate were eaten in Britain last year! The average person spent 89p a week on chocolate, and adults in their forties and fifties eat the most.

Tuesday January 29

✽ Two baby duck-billed platypuses, the first to be born in captivity in Australia for nearly 50yrs, emerge from burrows at the Warrawong wildlife sanctuary, Adelaide. They measure about 30cm long.

Wednesday January 30

✽ English Heritage publishes a register of more than 900 listed historic buildings in London that are at risk. They include Battersea Power Station, the Midland Hotel, St Pancras, the Round House, Chalk Farm and the Fire Station, Old Kent Road.

Thursday January 31

✽ Mountain roads in South Wales are badly affected by heavy snowfalls.

✽ Worcester cathedral reaches its £4 million appeal target for urgent repairs.

The Gulf War

January 16

Operation Desert Storm.
The US launches a series of air raids on Iraqi troops who continue to occupy Kuwait despite the UN deadline which expired on January 15.

February 28

US President Bush orders the Allied troops to cease fire, and Kuwait celebrates its liberation. As they left Kuwait, the Iraqis set fire to hundreds of oil wells.

Below: Prime Minister John Major is presented with a Russian Kaslashnikov rifle abandoned by an Iraqi soldier.

US Marines fire a Howitzer at Iraqi positions inside Kuwait

Kuwait's beaches are covered in oil

The Central Command Chief, 'Stormin' Norman Schwarzkopf, is greeted on his return home

Oil terminal burning

Burning oil wells

An oil covered cormorant

❄ FEBRUARY ❄

Brit Awards. Lisa Stansfield, Elton John, Sinead O'Connor, Michael Hutchence of INXS, The Cure

Friday February 1

❄ An earthquake in Afghanistan and Pakistan's North West Frontier province, measuring 6.8 on the Richter Scale, leaves more than 1,200 people dead.

❄ Surfers ride up the Bristol Channel towards Gloucester on the Severn Bore, but fail to break the 2½ mile record.

Saturday February 2

❄ The 3 week Jorvik Viking Festival of Jolablot starts in York today. It includes mock battles, Viking feasts and the burning of a longship funeral pyre on the river Ouse.

Sunday February 3

❄ Radar tracking stations all over the world monitor the 40 tonne Soviet *Salyut 7* space station as it loses orbit and prepares to re-enter Earth's atmosphere.

❄ The 45th annual Clowns' Service is held at Holy Trinity Church, Dalston.

Monday February 4

❄ BBC TV's Blue Peter raises a record £4,301,298 for Romanian orphanages, beating the £3,700,000 collected in 1979 for Cambodia.

Tuesday February 5

❄ Violinist, Nigel Kennedy, is named Showbusiness Personality of the Year at the Variety Club Awards at the London Hilton. Albert Finney wins best Actor and Amanda Donohoe is named Best Actress.

Wednesday February 6

❄ Bob Marley Day in Jamaica - part of the government's new policy to honour people who have made an 'outstanding contribution to the national culture'.

❄ Temperatures tumble to -10°C tonight. On the French Riviera it snows for the first time in 5yrs.

Thursday February 7

❄ The 40 tonne Soviet space station, *Salyut 7*, lands in Argentina, after splitting into 250 pieces as it re-enters Earth's atmosphere.

❄ The IRA fire a mortar bomb from a van in Whitehall into the garden of 10 Downing St, where the Prime Minister is chairing a meeting. The windows shatter but no-one is hurt.

Friday February 8

❄ Heavy snowfalls close schools, offices, shops and factories in the south of England.

❄ Temperatures in Bournemouth drop to -11°C, colder than Moscow. Blizzards in the north disrupt roads and railways, with 3.6m drifts in Greater Manchester.

Saturday February 9

❄ The Big Freeze continues causing commuter chaos all over the country. British Rail blames delays and breakdowns on the 'wrong kind of snow', which is lighter than normal.

Sunday February 10

✳ Lisa Stansfield and Elton John are named best British female and male pop stars at the Brit Awards at the Dominion Theatre, London. Irish singer, Sinead O'Connor, wins the best international female star award and Michael Hutchence, of the Australian group INXS, is named best international male star.

Monday February 11

✳ The British Amateur Skating Championships on Bury Fen, Cambs., are abandoned because the ice is too rutted.

✳ Terry Hands-Heart and Roger Orford set off in a 1933 Morgan three-wheeler from Edinburgh Castle at the start of the 2,896 km Monte Carlo Challenge Rally.

Tuesday February 12

✳ Shrove Tuesday. Traditional Pancake Races take place in Olney, Bucks., and Covent Garden, London.

✳ Shrovetide Football is played at Alnwick, Northumberland, Ashbourne, Derbyshire, and Atherstone, Warks.

Wednesday February 13

✳ First day of Lent.

✳ The Department of the Environment launches a new anti-litter campaign, with £10 spot fines and new litter wardens.

Thursday February 14

✳

✳ St Valentine's Day.

✳ The Variety Club's 'Gold Heart Day' appeal is launched to raise £5 million for children's hospitals.

Friday February 15

✳ Chinese Year of the Sheep starts today.

✳ Ex-Coldstream Guard, Sammy Taylor, who served as a stretcher-bearer in the Battle of the Somme in 1916, and was wounded at Ypres the following year, celebrates his 100th birthday at home nr Bath.

Saturday February 16

✳ A 19km oil slick threatens thousands of birds wintering at the Slimbridge Wildfowl Trust, Glos., when 27,276 litres of oil escapes from British Steel's Llanwern plant in Gwent.

✳ Anthony Steward (27) sets off from Cape Town to sail solo 41,351.3km around the world in an open yacht.

Sunday February 17

✳ Gerald Brazewell (77), of Nailsworth, Glos., rides his 1937 Royal Enfield motorbike 1,406km from Land's End to John O'Groats in 23hrs 40mins to raise money for the Gloucestershire Cloud Nine Fund for seriously ill children.

Monday February 18

✳ Beginning of National Prune Week

✳ The Sussex Wildlife Trust sets up a special helpline to rescue homeless frog spawn in Sussex, Kent, Hampshire and the Isle of Wight.

Tuesday February 19

✳ High tides in the Severn Estuary help to disperse the oil slick (see Feb 16) which has now killed thousands of birds. Shelducks, mute swans, great crested grebes, redshanks and reed buntings, wintering in the estuary, are still at risk.

Wednesday February 20

❋ At the Grammy ceremony in New York, the American arranger and bandleader, Quincy Jones, wins 7 awards. British pop star, Phil Collins, collects the award for Record of the Year (for *Another Day in Paradise*) while Irish singer, Sinead O'Connor, wins the Best Alternative Performance category

Thursday February 21

❋ Famous British prima ballerina, Dame Margot Fonteyn (71), dies in hospital in Panama City, Panama.

❋ Jeanne Louise Calment celebrates her 116th birthday at home in Arles in the south of France.

❋ Tropical cyclone Daphne hits the north Australian coast.

Friday February 22

❋ Helen Sharman (27) from Surbiton, Surrey, is chosen to be the first British astronaut. She will take part in a mission to the *Mir* space station in May with 2 Soviet cosmonauts.

Saturday February 23

❋ Prince Naruhito of Japan celebrates his 31st birthday and is formally proclaimed Crown Prince and heir to the 2,651-year-old Chrysanthemum Throne by his father, Emperor Akihito.

Sunday February 24

❋ Firemen rescue people trapped in their homes after the river Ure bursts its banks and floods the Yorkshire town of Boroughbridge.

❋ A flock of 100 sheep is rescued by boat in nearby Aldborough.

Monday February 25

❋ The Dyfed Wildlife Trust puts 200 concrete model puffins on Cardigan Island in an attempt to lure real puffins back. They deserted the island after rats from a sinking ship colonized it in the 1930s.

Tuesday February 26

❋ Sulaiman Ali Nashnush (48), of Libya, the second tallest man in the world at 2.44m according to the Guinness Book of Records, dies after a heart attack.

Wednesday February 27

❋ Overseas Development Minister, Linda Chalker, launches the 10th anniversary Water Aid appeal by carrying a calabash, a traditional African water container, across Westminster Bridge, London.

❋ St Joseph's Catholic College in Sydney changes its name to Pemulwuy Koori College and becomes the first Aboriginal high school in the world.

PEMULWUY KOORI COLLEGE

Thursday February 28

❋ US President, George Bush, announces a ceasefire in the Gulf War.

❋ Author, Roald Dahl, who died last November, leaves £2,833,940 in his will, which is published today.

Happy Birthday's of 1991

Switzerland is 700

Crufts Dog Show is 100

Sandhurst Military Academy is 250

Ordnance Survey is 200 *(see Stamp page)*

The Royal Veterinary College is 200

Punch magazine is 150

The Royal Society of Chemists is 150

The Royal Liverpool Philharmonic
Orchestra is 150

The Royal Aeronautical Society is 125

National Canine Defence League is 100

The Empire State Building,
New York, is 60

Sadlers Wells is 60

Sindy is 30

Cats is 10

Top 10 Names
(according to the Times newspaper)

Girls		Boys
Elizabeth	1	James
Louise	2	William
Charlotte	3	Alexander
Rose	4	Thomas
Emily	5	Edward
Alice	6	Charles
Alexandra	7	John
Sophie	8	George
Olivia	9	Michael
Emma	10	Henry

Top 10 Films of 1991 (MRIB)

1 Robin Hood: Prince of Thieves
2 Terminator 2: Judgement Day
3 Silence of the Lambs
4 Three Men and a Little Lady
5 Dances with Wolves
6 Home Alone
7 Sleeping with the Enemy
8 The Naked Gun 2.5
9 Kindergarten Cop
10 The Commitments

Macaulay Culkin in *Home Alone*

Arnold Schwarzenegger
in *Terminator 2: Judgement Day*

Kevin Costner in *Robin Hood,
Prince of Thieves*

MARCH

The Oscars. Kevin Costner's *Dances with Wolves* wins 7 awards, Jeremy Irons wins Best Actor, Nick Parke wins Best Animated Short

Friday March 1
✳ St David's Day.

✳ Prince William (8), pays his first official visit to Wales with the Prince and Princess of Wales. He attends a St David's Day service in Llandaff Cathedral and performs his first public duty - unveiling a slogan to promote European tourism in Cardiff.

Saturday March 2
✳ Swimmers all over the country take part in the 5,000 metre 1991 National Swimathon in aid of Childline and the British Sports Association for the Disabled.

Sunday March 3
✳ A freak whirlwind tears across 40km of west Wales, uprooting trees, ripping roofs off houses and overturning cars and caravans between Carew, nr Pembroke, and Llangynog, nr Carmarthen.

Monday March 4
✳ The Queen conducts an investiture ceremony at Buckingham Palace with a bandaged left hand. She was bitten while trying to stop a fight between the royal corgis at Windsor Castle yesterday.

Tuesday March 5
✳ The last 16 US cruise missiles leave Greenham Common air base in Berkshire to be destroyed in the Arizona desert. The women's peace camp, which celebrates its 10th birthday in September, will continue until the base is closed down.

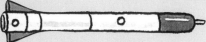

Wednesday March 6
✳ Dr George Carey is formally elected Archbishop of Canterbury.

✳ An estimated 5 million computers all over the world are affected by the Michelangelo virus which wipes the hard disk clean. It is named after the Renaissance painter, who was born today.

Thursday March 7
✳ An inquest at King's Lynn decides that the biggest hoard of gold and silver found this century, at Snettisham, Norfolk, is treasure trove and therefore the property of the crown. It includes bracelets, rings, coins and torcs that date back to the time of Queen Boadicea.

Friday March 8
✳ International Women's Day.

✳ Work grinds to a halt on the £4.6 million new sea wall at Lymington, Hants, when two small colonies of shrimp (*gammarus insensibilis*) and sea anenome (*nematostella vectensis*) are discovered. They are both protected species.

Saturday March 9
✳ Start of National Week of Sport.

✳ Oxfam ship, *Grain of Hope*, loads up with 5,000 tonnes of food aid at Ipswich before setting off for Africa where up to 20 million people face starvation because of the famine.

Sunday March 10

* Mothering Sunday.

* Prince Edward celebrates his 27th birthday with the help of a dozen friends and a large corgi-shaped cake, at a party in Knightsbridge, London.

Monday March 11

* Commonwealth Day.

* Nineteen journalists make the first train journey through the Channel tunnel at 22.5kph to inspect progress. They use the service tunnel, which has just been completed.

Tuesday March 12

* The Wall's Pocket Money Monitor shows a record 13% rise over the last year. The average pocket money nationwide for children, aged 5-16 years, is now £1.69p a week.

Wednesday March 13

* National No Smoking Day.

* McDonald's launches a new low-fat hamburger called the McLean. It contains only 10 grams of fat and 310 calories.

* The largest lever-operated signal box in Europe, the Severn Bridge box, near Shrewsbury station, is made a listed building.

Thursday March 14

* The Middleham Jewel, a gold and sapphire pendant dating from the reign of Richard III, goes on public display for the first time at the Yorkshire Museum, York. It was found 6yrs ago nr Middleham Castle, N. Yorks, and is valued at £2.5 million.

Friday March 15

* Comic Relief's third Red Nose Day. More than 9 million red plastic noses, with a pair of hands attached for the first time, are sold to raise money for famine relief and for charities in the UK.

Saturday March 16

* █████████

* Dublin formally takes over from Glasgow as the European Community's City of Culture.

* England's rugby team, captained by Will Carling, beats France 21-19 to win the Five Nations championship at Twickenham.

Sunday March 17

* St Patrick's Day.

* First day of Ramadan.

* The Dalai Lama, the spiritual leader of 6 million Tibetans, arrives in Britain at the start of a five-day visit.

Monday March 18

* The Princess of Wales buries a time capsule at the Hospital for Sick Children, Great Ormond Street. It contains a hologram of a snowflake, a solar-powered calculator, British coins, 5 tree seeds, a compact disc, a sheet of recycled paper, a European passport, a pocket TV, a copy of *The Times* newspaper and a photograph of herself.

Tuesday March 19

* Budget Day. Chancellor of the Exchequer, Norman Lamont, raises VAT to 17.5%.

* The Marlborough Maze, symbolizing the first Duke of Marlborough's victory at the Battle of Blenheim in 1704, opens at Blenheim Palace, Oxon.

Wednesday March 20

* BT launches its new £50 million red and blue 'prancing piper' logo.

* After winning a referendum on Soviet national unity, President Gorbachev announces that bread and meat prices will treble and that milk prices will double.

Thursday March 21

❋ Spring Equinox.

❋ Environment Minister, Michael Heseltine, announces that the unpopular community charge or poll tax will be replaced by a new local tax based on property and people.

Friday March 22

❋ Brazil suspends international coffee sales until further notice.

❋ The Royal Shakespeare Company re-opens its London base in the Barbican Centre, closed temporarily through lack of money, with a performance of *Love's Labours Lost*.

Saturday March 23

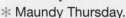

❋ The first letter to be sent through the post with a franked Penny Black stamp, on May 2, 1840, to Mr Blenkinsop, a locomotive engineer, of Bedlington Ironworks, nr Morpeth is sold for £1,340,000 at an auction in Lugano, Switzerland.

❋ Princess Eugenie of York celebrates her first birthday.

Sunday March 24

❋ The Soviet space station, *Mir*, recovers after a near miss with an unmanned *Progress-7* cargo craft. They come within 19km of colliding before ground control overrides the computer and changes the cargo craft's course.

Monday March 25

❋ At the Oscar ceremonies in Los Angeles, USA, Kevin Costner's film *Dances with Wolves* wins 7 awards, including Best Picture and Best Director. Jeremy Irons is named Best Actor (for *Reversal of Fortunes*) and Nick Parke, from Preston, wins an Oscar for Best Animated Short with *Creature Comforts*.

Tuesday March 26

❋ According to the Kennel Club's annual survey the Yorkshire terrier is now the most popular pedigree dog, followed by the Retriever, the German Shepherd and the West Highland White.

Wednesday March 27

❋ South Africa is granted conditional readmittance to the Olympic Games, after 30yrs absence, making it eligible for next year's games in Barcelona.

Thursday March 28

❋ Maundy Thursday.

❋ The Queen presents Maundy money (65p each) to pensioners at a special ceremony in Westminster Abbey.

❋ President Gorbachev brings out the troops in Moscow as more than 100,000 people demonstrate in favour of Boris Yeltsin, the radical leader and head of the Russian Federation.

Friday March 29

❋ Good Friday.

❋ The National Centre for Owl Conservation opens this week-end in Wolterton Park, nr Aylsham, Norfolk. The barn owl is now an endangered species with only an estimated 4,000 nesting pairs in England and Wales.

Saturday March 30

❋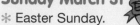

❋ First day of Passover.

❋ Oxford wins the 137th University Boat Race from Putney to Mortlake, beating Cambridge by 4¼ lengths, in a time of 16.59 mins.

Sunday March 31

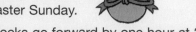

❋ Easter Sunday.

❋ Clocks go forward by one hour at 2am.

❋ A new brick and turf maze is officially opened at Parham Park, nr Pulborough, West Sussex. The design is based on the backcloth and coverlet of the Elizabethan bed in the house's great chamber.

❖ APRIL ❖

WWF launches worldwide campaign to stop the trade in rhino horn
New US space shuttle *Endeavour* unveiled

Monday April 1
❖ Bank Holiday.

❖ The world elver-eating contest at Frampton, Glos., is cancelled for the second year running because the price of baby eels has rocketed to £20 a kilo.

Tuesday April 2
❖ Belmarsh Prison, the first major jail to be built in London for a century, opens in Woolwich, south east London. It will have 850 inmates.

Wednesday April 3
❖ The Mayor of Pisa calls for help from the Italian government to save the Leaning Tower of Pisa, which has moved 1mm in the last 3 months.

❖ Author, Graham Greene (86), dies in hospital at Vevey, Switzerland.

Thursday April 4
❖ The Queen Mother opens the new £3 million Queen Mother stand at Aintree racecourse, Liverpool, the home of the Grand National.

Friday April 5
❖ US space shuttle *Atlantis* blasts off at the start of a 5-day mission, which will include the first American space walk since 1985 and the launch of the 17 tonne Gamma Ray observatory.

Saturday April 6
❖ Daffodil Day, in aid of Marie Curie Cancer Care.

❖ *Seagram* (12-1), ridden by Nigel Hawke, wins the Grand National at Aintree by 5 lengths from *Garrison Savannah*.

❖ England beats Spain 12-0 in the opening game of the first women's rugby World Cup at Swansea.

Sunday April 7
❖ In Kuwait, American firefighters put out the first of more than 500 blazing oil wells, which have been raging since the end of the Gulf War.

❖ Ian McKellan wins Actor of the Year at the Olivier Awards for his Duke of Gloucester in the RSC's *Richard III*.

Monday April 8
❖ London Zoo, which is threatened with closure, launches a nationwide appeal to raise £13 million.

❖ Two astronauts spend 6hrs outside the US shuttle *Atlantis*, manoeuvring equipment around in space, in preparation for the international space station which will be built later in the decade.

Tuesday April 9
❖ Patricia Scotland (35), a barrister at Gray's Inn, London, takes silk to become Britain's first black female Queen's Counsel.

❖ Georgia votes for freedom from the Soviet Union. It is the fourth of 15 republics to declare independence.

Wednesday April 10

❖ The Ministry of Agriculture warns that Colorado beetles, which can ruin potato crops, have been spotted in French parsley in Surrey, Spanish lettuces in Colchester, Essex, and in French lettuces in Brighton.

❖ Six fishermen are lost in the English Channel after their trawler, *Wilhelmina J*, collides in thick fog, with cargo ship, *Zulfikar*.

Thursday April 11

❖ Hottest day of the year so far. Temperatures reach 23 °C in Cromer, Norfolk.

❖ South Africa becomes the first country to declare the great white shark a protected species.

Friday April 12

❖ In New York, demonstrators picket the first night of the British musical, *Miss Saigon*, on Broadway, protesting that it is racist and sexist.

Saturday April 13

❖ A state of emergency is declared in the Bay of Genoa, Italy, as fire rages for the third day on board oil tanker *Haven*, carrying 143,000 tonnes of crude oil, which exploded off Pegli on Thursday.

Sunday April 14

❖ Twenty paintings by Van Gogh, worth hundreds of millions of pounds, are stolen from the Van Gogh Museum in Amsterdam. They are found, 2½ hrs later, in the getaway car.

Monday April 15

❖ A brass whistle, belonging to the third officer of the *Titanic* when she sank in 1912, is sold for £3,100 at an auction of memorabilia in London today, the 79th anniversary of the disaster. One of the ship's fire axes sells for £2,300.

Tuesday April 16

❖ English Nature announces that, after an 8yr breeding programme, which involved importing eggs and female butterflies from Sweden, the Large Blue butterfly has returned to parts of Devon.

❖ The famous film director, David Lean (83), who won 23 Oscars, dies in London.

Wednesday April 17

❖ Yellow Ribbon Day - thousands of ribbons flutter on trees and buildings as part of a campaign to remember British hostages still held in Beirut. A vigil is held at St Bride's Church, London, to mark the fifth anniversary of the kidnapping of journalist, John McCarthy.

Thursday April 18

❖ Watch out for the giant Himalayan Porcupine *(hystrix africaeustralis)* which has been spotted on Dartmoor recently. Also known as the crested porcupine, it has 30cm long quills which can cause serious injury.

Friday April 19

❖ Dr George Carey is enthroned as the103rd Archbishop of Canterbury.

❖ Fred Stahly, from Kirkcaldy, Fife, wins the Concours International du Meilleur Boudin (world black pudding championships) in Mortagne-au-Perche, Normandy.

Saturday April 20

❖ A sudden late frost nips the vine buds in Bordeaux and Champagne in France seriously damaging the prospects for this year's harvest. 400,000 bottles of wine will be lost.

Top Selling 45s of 1991

1. Everything I Do I Do It For You **Bryan Adams**
2. The Shoop Shoop Song **Cher**
3. I'm Too Sexy **Right Said Fred**
4. Do The Bartman **The Simpsons**
5. The One and Only **Chesney Hawkes**
6. Bohemian Rhapsody **Queen**
7. Any Dream Will Do **Jason Donovan**
8. I Wanna Sex You Up **Colour Me Badd**
9. 3AM Eternal **The KLF**
10. Don't Let The Sun Go Down On Me **George Michael & Elton John**

Top Ten LPs

1. Greatest Hits **The Eurythmics**
2. Greatest Hits II **Queen**
3. Stars **Simply Red**
4. Out of Time **REM**
5. Dangerous **Michael Jackson**
6. The Immaculate Collection **Madonna**
7. Love Hurts **Cher**
8. Seal **Seal**
9. From Time to Time **Paul Young**
10. The Very Best of Elton John **Elton John**

(New Musical Express)

Bryan Adams

Queen

Michael Jackson

Jason Donovan

Lisa Stanfield

Elton John at Watford FC

At the Brit Awards in February, Elton John and Lisa Stanfield were voted Best Male and Best Female singers. Michael Hutchence of INXS was voted Best International Male Singer, and Sinead O'Conner best International Female Singer

Michael Hutchence (INXS)

Sunday April 21

❖ 23,559 runners start the 11th London Marathon which, this year, incorporates the World Marathon Cup for the first time. Yakov Tolstikov, from Siberia, wins in 2hrs 9mins 17secs and Rosa Mota, of Portugal, is the fastest woman, with a time of 2hrs 26mins 14secs.

Monday April 22

❖ An army of 117,000 people begin collecting the 23 million Census forms which were sent out to every household in the land by the Office of Population Censuses and Surveys.

Tuesday April 23

❖ Yorkshire Water issues an amber warning after toxic blue-green algae is spotted in Scout Dyke Reservoir, nr Penistone, Yorks.

❖ The Queen holds a State Banquet at Windsor Castle in honour of the President of Poland, Lech Walesa, and his wife, at the start of their four-day state visit.

Wednesday April 24

❖ Children at Holly Hill Primary School, Selston, Notts, who have been taking part in a special NASA experiment to grow tomatoes from seeds that spent 6yrs in space, are ordered to destroy their plants as the Ministry of Agriculture fears that they might carry a virus that could destroy potato crops.

Thursday April 25

❖ A swimsuit, worn by Marilyn Monroe in the 1954 film *There's No Business Like Showbusiness*, is sold for £103,200 at Christie's, London.

❖ WWF launches a worldwide campaign to stop the trade in rhino horn.

Friday April 26

❖ The new US space shuttle *Endeavour* is unveiled at Palmdale, California, USA. Capable of spending a month in orbit with a crew of 8 people, it is the most advanced manned spaceship so far and will make its maiden flight next year. It has flushing lavatories that are guaranteed not to clog up.

Saturday April 27

❖ A rally is held in Trafalgar Square, London, in aid of World Day for Laboratory Animals.

❖ A rare Sardinian warbler, usually found in the Mediterranean, is seen nr Weybourne, Norfolk.

Sunday April 28

❖ The US space shuttle *Discovery* blasts off from Cape Canaveral, Florida, on an 8-day mission, which is part of the Pentagon's Star Wars programme.

❖ Pop singer, Michael Jackson, signs a multi-media deal with Sony this month that makes him the highest paid entertainer in the world.

Monday April 29

❖ A powerful earthquake measuring 7.2 on the Richter Scale, devastates the Soviet republic of Georgia.

❖ The Princess Royal launches the Save the Children Fund's 'Skip a Lunch - Save a Life' appeal for Africa.

Tuesday April 30

❖ The worst cyclone for 20 years leaves 125,000 people dead and 10 million homeless in Bangladesh. It roars across the Bay of Bengal at 232kph, driving a 6m high tidal wave into the port of Chittagong.

❈ MAY ❈

The Simple Truth pop concert at Wembley in aid of Kurdish refugees
Helen Sharman blasts off to become first British astronaut

Wednesday May 1

❈ The 381m, 102-storey, Empire State Building celebrates its 60th birthday in New York. Guest of honour at the party is the actress, Fay Wray, who appeared in the first *King Kong* film, which was made in 1933.

Thursday May 2

❈ Launch of National Pet Week.

❈ The Marylebone Cricket Club (MCC) votes to uphold its ban on women after Rachel Heyhoe-Flint, former women's team captain, tries to join.

Friday May 3

❈ Members of the Sherlock Holmes Society of London make a pilgrimage to Switzerland for a re-enactment of the detective's famous last battle with Moriarty, above the Reichenbach Falls, nr Meiringen. The date for Holmes' apparent death in *The Final Problem* was May 4, 1891.

Saturday May 4

❈ A train breakdown delays the Queen's arrival at the Gulf War Service of Remembrance in Glasgow Cathedral.

❈ Sweden wins the 36th Eurovision Song contest in Rome with *Captured by a Love Storm.*

Sunday May 5

❈ A meteorite, weighing more than 500kg, lands in a garden at Glatton, nr Peterborough, still warm after hurtling through the atmosphere. It is the first meteorite to be found in Britain since 1969.

Monday May 6

❈ Bank Holiday - the wettest in the south of England on record!

❈ Miss Gale Force Wind wins the Alternative Miss World Competition at the Business Design Centre, Islington.

❈ US space shuttle *Discovery* lands in Florida when high winds force the astronauts to make a 4827km detour from the target landing site in California.

Tuesday May 7

❈ No Entry to Weybourne beach, Norfolk, after 2 tanker trailers containing 24,000 litres of toxic chemicals, are washed ashore. More than 1,000 people have been evacuated because of the poisonous fumes.

Wednesday May 8

❈ The Queen opens ITN's new headquarters in Grays Inn Road, London.

❈ English Heritage unveils £10 million plans for preserving Stonehenge in Wiltshire and restoring the site to its original appearance.

Thursday May 9

❈ 44th Cannes International Film Festival opens in the south of France.

❈ David Griffiths (28) and Phil Barber (31) break the world abseiling record by descending 267.8m from Britain's tallest TV mast at Emley Moor, nr Huddersfield, W. Yorks.

Friday May 10

✤ The fruit and vegetable market at Spitalfields in London closes today after more than 300yrs. It moves from Bishopsgate, just outside the old City wall, to a new £60 million purpose-built complex at Leyton, East London.

Saturday May 11

✤ Andrew Lloyd Webber's musical *Cats* celebrates its 10th birthday at the New London Theatre. The cast has used up 2,600 pairs of shoes and 2,300 costumes.

Sunday May 12

✤ Rod Stewart launches a pop concert The Simple Truth, at Wembley which raises £57 million in aid of Kurdish refugees. Singers, including Chris de Burgh, M C Hammer, Whitney Houston and Paul Simon, perform in front of a 12,000 strong audience. A worldwide audience of 50 million watches on TV.

Monday May 13

✤ Beginning of Christian Aid Week.

✤ The RSPB announces that England's only pair of breeding golden eagles have hatched a chick in the Haweswater reserve in the Lake District.

Tuesday May 14

✤ The Queen arrives in the USA on her first State visit since 1976. She will watch her first baseball match tomorrow - in Baltimore stadium - and address a joint meeting of the US Congress on Thursday.

Wednesday May 15

✤ Manchester United, captained by Bryan Robson, wins the European Cup Winners' Cup in Rotterdam, defeating Barcelona 2-1.

It marks the return of England to European football after a 6yr ban, following the Heysel stadium disaster in 1985.

Thursday May 16

✤ President Mitterand appoints Edith Cresson (57) the first woman Prime Minister of France.

✤ A stretch of the main Paddington to Penzance railway in Somerset is closed after a derailed freight train, carrying petrol, kerosene and diesel oil, explodes near Taunton.

Friday May 17

✤ An American lark sparrow is seen in the Norfolk village of Waxham, - only the second recorded sighting in Britain.

✤ The fourth biggest sapphire in the world, weighing 337.66 carats, is sold for £1,330,645 at Christie's, Geneva.

Saturday May 18

✤ Tottenham Hotspur wins the FA Cup for a record eighth time at Wembley, beating Nottingham Forest 2-1.

✤ Helen Sharman, the first British astronaut, blasts off from Baikonur, USSR, with 2 Soviet cosmonauts in a *Soyuz* space craft, on an 8-day mission to the *Mir* space station.

Sunday May 19

✤ British Tourist Authority's annual survey shows that Mme Tussaud's is still the top paying tourist attraction, followed by the Tower of London, Alton Towers, the Natural History Museum and Chessington World of Adventure.

Monday May 20

✤ British astronaut, Helen Sharman, talks to Soviet President, Mikhail Gorbachev, on the telephone from the *Mir* space station before sitting down to a meal of tinned tuna, dried cheese, an apple and fruit juice from a tube.

The Royal Family

1 **March 1: Prince William (8)**, pays his first official visit to Wales with his parents.

2 **May 14: The Queen** in the USA with President Bush.

3 **June 3: Prince William** leaving Great Ormond Street Hospital, where he had 24 stitches in his head after he was hit with a golf club at school.

4 **September 11: Princess Beatrice (3)** spends her first day at nursery school. She is pictured arriving with her mother, the Duchess of York.

5 **October 23: Prince William (now 9)** and **Prince Harry (7)** arriving in Toronto, Canada at the start of their first official overseas visit with their parents.

6 **July 30:** A rain-soaked **Prince and Princess of Wales** greet the Italian tenor Luciano Pavarotti after his free concert in Hyde Park.

Top 10 Names in Forbes Magazine's

Annual List of World's Highest Paid Entertainers plus estimated earnings for 1990 and 1991

1 New Kids on the Block ($115m)

2 William H. Cosby ($113m)

3 Oprah Winfrey ($80m)

4 Madonna ($63m)

5 Michael Jackson ($60m)

6 Kevin Costner ($59m)

7 Johnny Carson ($55m)

8 The Rolling Stones ($55m)

9 Charles M. Schulz ($51m)

10 Steven Spielberg ($50m)

Michael Jackson

NKOTB

The Rolling Stones

Tuesday May 21

✣ Warmest day of the year 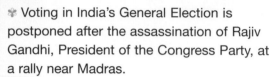 so far - it's 24.6°C in London.

✣ Voting in India's General Election is postponed after the assassination of Rajiv Gandhi, President of the Congress Party, at a rally near Madras.

Wednesday May 22

✣ At 10.30am the 183m long French Tunnel Boring Machine, nicknamed 'Europa', breaks through from the French to the English side in the north running train tunnel, 46m under the English Channel. The first service tunnel was completed last December.

Thursday May 23

✣ Experts at the Museum of London examine an 8th century skeleton, which was discovered yesterday under 6m of mud on the Thames foreshore. Some bones are missing from the right hand and there is a small hole in the head thought to have been caused by trepanning.

Friday May 24

✣ Coastguards warn swimmers of a plague of lesser octopuses (Octopus eledone) along the coasts of Dorset and Devon. They have 60cm-long tentacles and can give a nasty bite with their beak-like mouths.

Saturday May 25

✣ King's College School, Cambridge, celebrates its 550th birthday. It was founded in 1441 by Henry VII, a year after its sister school, Eton.

Sunday May 26

✣ British astronaut, Helen Sharman, returns to Earth after her 8-day mission to Soviet space station *Mir*. She is accompanied by Soviet cosmonauts Musa Manarov and Viktor Afanasyev, who have been in space since last year.

Monday May 27

✣ Bank Holiday.

✣ Greenpeace delivers to the Japanese embassy in London a 2 tonne stone memorial to the 6,690 whales killed by Japan since the 1986 international ban on commercial whaling.

Tuesday May 28

✣

✣ Tens of thousands of mourners watch as the ashes of Rajiv Gandhi, who was assassinated a week ago, are scattered by his son, Rahul, into India's holiest river, the Ganges.

Wednesday May 29

✣ The European Commission decides to blow up its headquarters, the Berlaymont building in Brussels, because it is riddled with toxic asbestos powder. Officials will move to other EC buildings in Brussels later in the week.

Thursday May 30

✣ Pigs are banned from the Suffolk Show, which opened yesterday, after an outbreak of blue ear disease.

✣ Two large oil slicks along the west coast of Shetland, threaten colonies of nesting puffins, skuas and kittiwakes on the island of Foula.

Friday May 31

✣ Iceland withdraws from the International Whaling Commission in Reykjavik after a decision to continue a conditional ban on commercial whaling for another 5yrs.

❀ JUNE ❀

Mt Pinatubo in Philippines starts erupting and keeps going for months, affecting the weather worldwide

Saturday June 1

❀ British musical *Miss Saigon* wins two Tony awards in New York. Jonathan Pryce wins Best Leading Actor in a musical and Lea Salonga is named Best Leading Actress in a musical. Nigel Hawthorne is voted Best Leading Actor in a play for his performance in *Shadowlands*.

Sunday June 2

❀ Stephen Allen, an actor from Lancaster, wins BBC's Mastermind competition. His specialist subject is the life and voyages of Sir Francis Drake.

Monday June 3

❀ Prince William (8) has 24 stitches in his head at Great Ormond Street Hospital for Sick Children. He suffered a depressed fracture of the skull when he was accidentally hit by a golf club at his prep school in Berkshire.

Tuesday June 4

❀ Launch of National Sleep-Out Week.

❀ The volcano at Mount Fugen in Japan erupts after being dormant for 200yrs. It sends a 200kph avalanche of molten lava down the mountain, setting fire to houses and forests.

Wednesday June 5

❀ World Environment Day.

❀ The US space shuttle, *Columbia*, takes off with 7 astronauts, 29 white rats and 2,478 jellyfish on board. It is the 41st shuttle mission, but the first dedicated to biological research.

Thursday June 6

❀ A new smaller £20 note is issued this week. It measures 80mm x 149mm, and shows the famous scientist, Sir Michael Faraday (1791-1867).

Friday June 7

❀ The European Space Agency's experimental £487 million communications satellite, *Olympus*, launched in July 1989, is now thousands of kms off course, after contact with ground control is lost and the batteries run down.

Saturday June 8

❀ A record 35 British beaches are awarded the European Blue Flag for cleanliness this week.

❀ Billy Bunter books, by Frank Richards, are banned from libraries in Lincolnshire because they are too old-fashioned.

Sunday June 9

❀ England's cricket captain, Graham Gooch, scores an undefeated 154 runs in one innings at Headingley against the West Indies. England goes on to win the Test Match, beating the West Indies at home for the first time in 22yrs.

Monday June 10

❀ Almost 6,000 tonnes of tickertape showers down on the victory parade of Gulf War soldiers in New York. They march down Broadway, which has been known as the Canyon of Heroes since the first tickertape parade for Teddy Roosevelt in 1910.

Tuesday June 11

✿ The last section of the new Dartford - Thurrock bridge on the M25 is lowered into position. It is the first road bridge to be built over the Thames downstream of the City of London since Tower Bridge in 1894.

Wednesday June 12

✿

✿ Pete Townshend, guitarist with *The Who* rock group for 27yrs, is officially declared a Living Legend at the 3rd International Rock Awards in London Arena. Madonna receives the People's Choice award.

Thursday June 13

✿ A huge eruption at the Mount Pinatubo volcano in the Philippines blots out the sun and covers the countryside with a thick layer of ash. Tens of thousands of people are evacuated. The volcano has been dormant for more than 600yrs.

Friday June 14

✿ American athlete, Leroy Burrell, beats Carl Lewis to set a new 100m world record of 9.90secs at the National Championships in New York.

Saturday June 15

✿ The Queen's Official Birthday.

✿ In the Birthday Honours List actress Gwen Ffrangcon-Davies (100), is made a Dame.

✿ Motor bikes from all over the world roar into Cheltenham racecourse for the first ever Harley Owners Group (HOG) European Festival.

Sunday June 16

✿ Fathers' Day.

✿ Annual Commons versus Lords tug o'war championship in aid of the Cancer Relief Macmillan Fund.

✿ More than 35,000 people take part in the 16th annual London to Brighton cycle race in aid of the British Heart Foundation.

Monday June 17

✿ Apartheid in South Africa officially ends today with the repeal of the Population Registration Act.

✿ *Robin Hood: Prince of Thieves*, starring Kevin Costner, takes $26 million (£16 million) at the box office in its first 3 days in the USA.

Tuesday June 18

✿ Chiharu Sakai (29), from Philadelphia, USA, wins the final of the World Piano Competition at the Royal Festival Hall, London.

✿ Shimetaro Hara, the oldest man in Japan, dies aged 108.

Wednesday June 19

✿ One of Britain's rarest plants, the Badgeworth buttercup (*Ranunculus ophioglossifolius*) is in bloom at a small nature reserve nr Cheltenham, Glos.

✿ Police seal off the roads to Stonehenge, Wilts, in an effort to stop hippies congregating there to celebrate the summer solstice on Friday.

Thursday June 20

✿ 39 nations, meeting in Madrid, sign a Treaty agreeing that Antarctica will be declared 'a continent for peace and science'. They also decide to ban huskies from Antarctica because of the danger of imported disease.

Friday June 21

✿ Longest day of the year.

✿ Summer solstice.

✿ A team of Japanese physicists gathers in Wiltshire at the start of a 5-week corn circle watch.

✿ Prince William celebrates his 9th birthday at home where he is recovering after an operation *(see June 3)*.

Saturday June 22

✿ Manager, Terry Venables, and businessman, Alan Sugar, sign a £7.25 million deal to take over Tottenham Hotspur Football Club.

✿ Lisa Gasteen (Aus), wins the 1991 Cardiff Singer of the World competition.

Sunday June 23

✿ Phil Appleby, of Leamington Spa, wins the National Scrabble Championships in London.

✿ Indonesia wins the International Dragon Boat Festival race in Hong Kong harbour, completing a 630m course in 2mins 32.29secs. Britain's only competitors, the Hartlepool Powermen, capsize after 400m.

Monday June 24

✿ Midsummer Day.

✿ Torrential rain wipes out any play on the opening day of the Wimbledon Lawn Tennis Championships.

✿ Cinema Day in France: international film stars leave their handprints in wet cement at the Arche de Defense in Neuilly, Paris.

Tuesday June 25

✿ Blue ear pig disease spreads to Norfolk.

✿ Fleet Street is sold for £16,000, Threadneedle Street for £12,000 and the Old Bailey for £5,500 at a sale of street signs from the Corporation of London at Guildhall.

Wednesday June 26

✿ Former prime minister Margaret Thatcher receives the Honorary Freedom of the City of Westminster at a ceremony at the Banqueting House, Whitehall.

Thursday June 27

✿ Fierce fighting erupts in Yugoslavia when Slovenia and Croatia declare independence.

✿ Only 52 matches have been completed so far in the wettest Wimbledon championships ever. Andre Agassi (USA), obeys Wimbledon's strict dress code and wears white in his opening match against Grant Connell (Can).

Friday June 28

✿ Paul McCartney's first classical work, Liverpool Oratorio, is performed in Liverpool Cathedral by the Royal Liverpool Philharmonic Orchestra, conducted by Carl Davis.

Saturday June 29

✿ The Royal Mint issues a special medal this week to celebrate the 500th anniversary of Henry VIII's birth. 5,000 bronze medals are struck at £42.50 each and 2,500 silver ones at £85 each.

Sunday June 30

✿ It has been so wet, and so many matches have been cancelled, that tennis is played for the first time ever on the middle Sunday of the Wimbledon Lawn Tennis Championships.

☀ JULY ☀

It's a Wash Out! Torrential rain ruins Wimbledon, the Test Match and Pavarotti's concert in Hyde Park

Monday July 1

☀ The Princess of Wales celebrates her 30th birthday.

☀ The use of rear seat belts in cars is compulsory from today with the exception of passengers in royal processions, milk floats and delivery vans.

Tuesday July 2

☀ Trade and Industry Secretary, Peter Lilley, confirms that miles, yards, feet and inches will remain despite threats from Brussels. Milk will still be delivered in pint bottles and beer will still be drunk in pints, rather than in 0.568 litres.

Wednesday July 3

☀ Jennifer Capriati (15), the youngest player in this year's Wimbledon tennis tournament, beats fellow American and nine times champion, Martina Navratilova (34), 6-4, 7-5. John McEnroe (USA), is fined £6,250 for 'verbal attack' on an official.

Thursday July 4

☀ US Independence Day.

☀ There are spectacular meteor displays tonight! One splashes down in the Bristol Channel and only just misses a tug.

Friday July 5

☀ Record pollen levels cause an outbreak of sneezing all over the country. In Cardiff the count reaches 365, Warwick 348, Isle of Wight 318 and Salford 305.

 ah chooo!

Saturday July 6

☀ Steffi Graf (Ger) wins the women's singles title at Wimbledon, beating Gabriela Sabatini (Arg), 6-4, 3-6, 8-6.

☀ The start of the 3,861km Tour de France cycle race in Lyons. It will finish on July 28 in Paris.

Sunday July 7

☀ Michael Stich (Ger), beats his fellow countryman, Boris Becker, to win the men's singles title at Wimbledon 6-4, 7-6, 6-4.

☀ English motor racing driver, Nigel Mansell, wins the French Grand Prix and overtakes Stirling Moss's record 16 grand prix victories.

Monday July 8

☀ British Rail launches the new InterCity 225 service from London to Edinburgh. It makes the 632km journey in 4hrs 8mins, cutting 30mins off the previous fastest time.

Tuesday July 9

☀ With the end of apartheid in South Africa, the International Olympic Committee re-admits South Africa as a member, and invites them to take part in next years games in Barcelona.

☀ The Queen opens the new Sainsbury Wing of the National Gallery, London.

Sports Personalities

World Athletic Championships Tokyo

August - September

1. Liz McColgan wins gold in the womens 10,000m.
2. Kriss Akabusi wins the last leg of the mens relay.
3. Mike Powell breaks the world long jump record.
4. Leroy Burrell in the 200m.
5. Carl Lewis sets a new world record winning the 100m in 9.86secs.

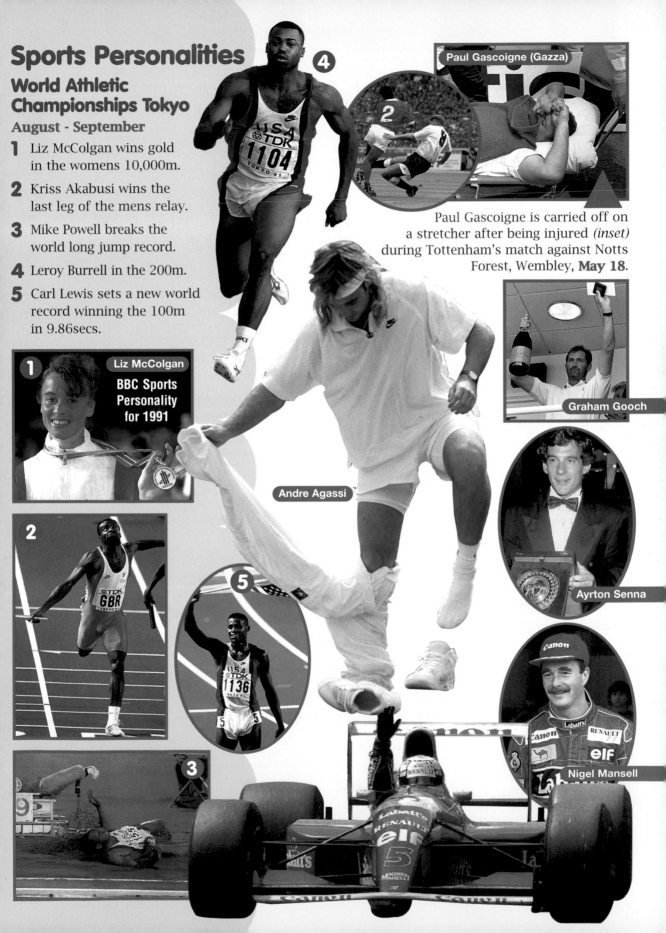

Paul Gascoigne (Gazza)

Paul Gascoigne is carried off on a stretcher after being injured *(inset)* during Tottenham's match against Notts Forest, Wembley, **May 18**.

1 **Liz McColgan**

BBC Sports Personality for 1991

Graham Gooch

Andre Agassi

Ayrton Senna

Nigel Mansell

Wednesday July 10

* The International Cricket Council votes to re-admit South Africa to Test cricket.

* Yorkshire Cricket Club announces that it will allow overseas players and Englishmen not born in Yorkshire to play for the county.

Thursday July 11

* The day of two dawns: thousands of people arrive in Hawaii to watch a total solar eclipse, which lasts about 4mins. It is the last total solar eclipse in the western hemisphere until the year 2,017.

Friday July 12

* Thames Water announces a £810 million modernisation plan for London's sewers which includes new pumping stations, computerisation and a flood alleviation scheme.

Saturday July 13

* Islamic New Year (AH1412)

* A torchlight procession and firework display in Milford Haven celebrates the start of the Cutty Sark Tall Ships race. The 100 strong fleet will set off for Cork, Belfast and Aberdeen before crossing the North Sea to the Netherlands.

Sunday July 14

* Bastille Day in France.

* The Princess Royal opens the World Student Games in Sheffield, and British astronaut, Helen Sharman, lights the flame. About 6,000 athletes from 111 nations will take part.

Monday July 15

* St Swithin's Day.

* A huge copper statue of Nike, the Greek goddess of victory, is reinstalled on top of the Brandenburg Gate, Berlin, after a £100,000 renovation.

* A gigantic corn circle is spotted at Alton Barnes, Wilts., exactly a year to the day since it last appeared there.

Tuesday July 16

* Water flows in the Trevi Fountain, Rome, for the first time in 3yrs, after a £1.4 million restoration.

* A spectacular banquet, firework display and laser show at Buckingham Palace welcomes members of the Group of Seven (G7) countries meeting in London this week.

Wednesday July 17

* The 2.5 tonne European Remote Sensing satellite, the *ERS-1*, goes into orbit 772km above Earth. It is Europe's first environmental satellite, and will monitor pollution, the destruction of the rain forests and the size of polar ice caps.

Thursday July 18

* Project Urquhart begins a 4yr programme to measure and map the depths of Loch Ness in Scotland. It is the first serious biological study of the waters, and might just solve the mystery of the Loch Ness Monster.

Friday July 19

* A Honda team wins the Shell Mileage Marathon at Silverstone race track, with a fuel consumption of 9,882km per 4.5 litres.

* A crisp shortage looms because the wet weather has delayed the potato harvest.

Saturday July 20

* A snail called Streaker sets a new record at the World Snail Racing Championships at Congham, Norfolk. He completes a 33cm course in 2mins 22secs.

Sunday July 21

* Tribute to Bob Marley - a festival commemorating the 10th anniversary the great reggae singer's death in 1981 - is held at the West London Stadium.

Monday July 22

* The Citizen's Charter is launched by Prime Minister, John Major.

* More than 70 different measures are introduced to raise the quality of public services, including maximum waiting times for NHS operations.

Tuesday July 23

* Eruptions at Mount Pinatubo in the Philippines have now lasted 40 days. So far, more than 435 people have been killed and a quarter of a million have been left homeless.

Wednesday July 24

* Canary Wharf, the London Docklands development which includes Britain's tallest building, opens to the public for the first time today.

Thursday July 25

* Tottenham Hotspur football club signs a £5.5 million deal for the transfer of Paul Gascoigne (Gazza) to the Italian club, Lazio.

Friday July 26

* Gigantic corn circles appear in a field near Netze in central Germany and in Grasdorf, south of Hanover. Visitors pay a 99 pfenning (35p) entrance fee to see them.

Saturday July 27

* Miguel Indurain (27), from Pamplona, Spain, wins the 21st stage of the Tour de France cycle race completing the 57km individual time trial in 1hr 11mins 45secs.

He will be declared overall winner of the race tomorrow in Paris.

Sunday July 28

* National Refugee Day.

* Nigel Mansell wins the German Grand Prix at Hockenheim and becomes the first British racing driver to complete a hat trick of grand prix victories since Jackie Stewart, 20yrs ago.

Monday July 29

* The Prince and Princess of Wales celebrate their 10th or tin wedding anniversary.

* The RSPB announces that the chick, hatched by England's only breeding pair of golden eagles, has flown safely from the nest at Haweswater, Cumbria.

Tuesday July 30

* The St John Ambulance brigade treats 193 people for cold during a free open-air concert given by Italian tenor, Luciano Pavarotti, in Hyde Park, London, in torrential rain.

* Blackpool Tower which, at only 158m, is the shortest member of the World Federation of Great Towers, celebrates the 100th anniversary of the laying of its foundation stone. Modelled on the Eiffel Tower, it cost £42,000 to build, and opened in May 1894.

Wednesday July 31

* America wins 39 gold, 20 silver and 20 bronze medals at the end of the World Wheelchair Games at Aylesbury, Bucks. Britain is runner-up with 37 gold, 38 silver and 26 bronze medals.

AUGUST

Terminator 2: Judgement Day, the most expensive film ever made, opens in London

British hostage John McCarthy released by Islamic Jihad

Thursday August 1

US President, George Bush, and Soviet Premier, Mikhail Gorbachev, sign the Strategic Arms Reduction Treaty (START), which will cut their nuclear weapons by up to a third, using pens made out of scrapped missiles.

Friday August 2

The European Space Agency's *Olympus* communications satellite *(see June 7)*, is back on course. Its batteries have been recharged by thousands of commands sent via tracking stations all over the world.

Saturday August 3

More than 4,500 athletes from 39 North and South American countries arrive in Cuba for the 11th Pan American Games.

Coastguards warn swimmers to beware poisonous jellyfish and stingrays sighted off Plymouth, Devon.

Sunday August 4

Happy 91st Birthday to Queen Elizabeth the Queen Mother. A special decorative gate in Hyde Park, made out of stainless steel, titanium and bronze, has been commissioned in her honour.

Monday August 5

Soichiro Honda (84), founder of the Japanese motor car manufacturing firm, dies in Tokyo. He set up his first company in 1946, making motorcycles.

Soviet pole vaulter, Sergei Bubka, sets a new outdoor world record of 6.10m at the Grand Prix meeting in Malmo, Sweden.

Tuesday August 6

Mrs Einir Jones, of Ammanford, Dyfed, is crowned Bard at the the Royal National Eisteddfod of Wales. She is only the third woman this century to win the honour.

Wednesday August 7

US astronauts on board space shuttle *Atlantis*, which was launched on Friday, will study the body's reaction to space. Col. James Adamson successfully squirts eyedrops into his eyes despite zero gravity.

Thursday August 8

Newly released British journalist, John McCarthy, who was held hostage by Islamic Jihad in Beirut, Lebanon, for 1,943 days (5 years 3 months), arrives back at RAF Lyneham, Wilts,

Friday August 9

About 150 hot air balloons, including Rupert Bear and several beer cans, take part in the Bristol Balloon Fiesta, which starts today.

Saturday August 10

The 17th World Scout Jamboree takes place in pouring rain in Korea. 20,000 Scouts from all over the world, including 1,400 from Britain, take part.

IRA Bomb in Whitehall, London

Mt Pinatubo erupts in Philippines

Robert Maxwell

February 7 Black smoke spirals from a white van in Whitehall. The IRA fired a bomb at 10 Downing Street from the van. Luckily nobody was hurt

November 5 Newspaper tycoon Robert Maxwell falls from his yacht and drowns while cruising in the Canaries

Sunnie & Jackie Mann

Maastricht

December 10 Douglas Hurd (left) and John Major pictured after the EEC summit at Maastricht where European leaders reached agreement on closer political and economic unity

Terry Waite

Hostages

Three British hostages, held in the Lebanon by Islamic Jihad, are released

Left: Journalist John McCarthy, released on **August 8**, who had been held for 1934 days

Top: Jackie Mann, pictured with his wife Sunnie, released on **September 25**, after 865 days

Above Right: Terry Waite, released on **November 18** after 1763 days

December 31: All the British hostages, including Brian Keenan, who was released last August, receive CBEs in the New Year's Honours list

John McCarthy

Sunday August 11

☀ Antonio Madonia, of Germany, wins first prize in the International Birdman Competition at Bognor Regis, Sussex. He flies 32m from the end of the pier.

Monday August 12

☀ Look out for the famous Perseid meteor shower tonight as Earth encounters millions of tiny fragments from the tail of Comet Swift-Tuttle. It's particularly easy to see this year because there is no light from the Moon.

Tuesday August 13

☀ More than 2,000 rush hour passengers are trapped on London tube trains for up to 2hrs, after a fire at Bank station on the Circle line.

☀ Jack Ryan (65), who invented the Barbie doll in 1959, dies in Los Angeles.

Wednesday August 14

☀ A 4,232 sq m picture of Van Gogh's Sunflowers blooms in a field at Heriot, nr Duns, in the Scottish borders. It is made up of 250,000 seedlings that were planted last month.

Thursday August 15

☀ More than 750,000 people hear singer songwriter, Paul Simon, sing in Central Park, New York, this evening. It's the first free open-air concert by a major star in the city for nearly 8yrs.

Friday August 16

☀ The coffin of Frederick the Great, King of Prussia, who died in 1786, is taken from Hohenzollern Castle, nr Hechingen, SE Germany, to Potsdam. It will be reinterred there, at Sans Souci Palace, where Frederick asked to be buried 205yrs ago.

Saturday August 17

☀ *Terminator 2: Judgement Day* opens in London. At an estimated cost of £60 million, it is the most expensive film ever made, with its star, Arnold Schwarzenegger, being paid more than £9 million.

Sunday August 18

☀ Hurricane Bob screams up the east coast of America at 145kph, causing serious damage in Cape Cod, Mass., and killing 16 people.

☀ Norman Maclean, of Edinburgh, wins the British Crossword Championships in record time, solving a 352 clue puzzle in 19½ mins. MACLEAN

Monday August 19

☀ The specialists are called in to rescue a colony of great crested newts living on the route of a new by-pass round Wymondham, nr Norwich. A special walkway will be built into a bridge to let the newts cross safely.

Tuesday August 20

☀ Monsoon rains in the Philippines trigger a huge avalanche of mud and rock from the Mount Pinatubo volcano, which has been erupting since June. More than 500 people have been killed in 11 weeks of violent activity.

Wednesday August 21

☀ Thousands of huge jellyfish, some more than 60cm wide, close down Hunterston nuclear power station on the Firth of Clyde, Scotland, for more than 24hrs when they get sucked into the filters.

Thursday August 22

☀ At a sale of rock and roll memorabilia at Sotheby's, London, two pieces of a guitar smashed by Jimi Hendrix in 1967, fetch £29,700, and a black sequinned jacket worn by Michael Jackson is sold for £11,000.

Friday August 23

☀ Top performers at this year's three-day Reading Festival, which starts today, include Iggy Pop and the Sisters of Mercy.

☀ British rock band, Dire Straights, start a 3yr world tour at The Point, Dublin.

Saturday August 24

☀ More than 600 fans from all over the country congregate in Manchester this weekend for the 32nd Star Trek Convention, celebrating the 25th anniversary of the original television series, starring William Shatner and Leonard Nimoy.

Sunday August 25

☀ At the World Track and Field Championships in Tokyo, American athlete, Carl Lewis, sets a new 100m world record with a time of 9.86secs. It is the fastest ever 100m race with six competitors finishing in under 10secs.

Monday August 26

☀ Bank Holiday.

☀ 5,000 teddies take part in the British Teddy Bear Festival in Kensington, London.

☀ Jack Lammiman, of Whitby, is summoned to appear before the magistrates after sailing more than 4,800km to the Arctic Circle in a fishing boat deemed unseaworthy. The 24-day journey commemorated the voyage of a Whitby whaling captain 200yrs ago.

Tuesday August 27

☀ Kriss Akabusi wins Britain's first medal (bronze) at the World Championships in Tokyo, with a time of 47.86 secs in the 400m hurdles.

Wednesday August 28

☀ Sarah Bell (4), of Ambleside, Cumbria, beats 24,000 other contestants to win the 34th Miss Pears title at the Savoy Hotel, London.

Thursday August 29

☀ A hand-made Christmas card, sent by John Lennon to his first wife, Cynthia, fetches £8,800 at a Christie's sale in London. His address book is sold for £3,850. A 1958 Buddy Holly poster is sold for £770.

Friday August 30

☀ Liz McColgan (27), from Scotland, wins the 10,000m and Britain's first gold medal at the Tokyo World Championships. Mike Powell (USA), sets a new world long jump record of 8.95m, shattering the longest-standing world record set by Bob Beamon (USA) in 1968.

Saturday August 31

☀ The tail end of Hurricane Bob blows into Britain, bringing cold weather and thunderstorms.

☀ 400 competitors from all over the world take part in the Portsmouth Triathlon: a 1500m sea swim followed by a 40km cycle race and a 10km run.

🍎 SEPTEMBER 🍎

Frozen body of man, 4000 years old, found in Similaun Glacier, Austria

Sunday September 1

🍃 National Disaster Day in Japan to commemorate the country's worst earthquake in 1923.

🍃 At the World Track and Field Championships in Tokyo, British athletes win the 4 x 400m relay race and set a new European record of 2mins 57.53secs.

Monday September 2

🍃 John Goodbody (48), sports correspondent of *The Times*, swims the English Channel from Dover to Cap Blanc Nez in 15hrs 40mins. He is the 407th person to complete the crossing since Captain Matthew Webb 116yrs ago.

Tuesday September 3

🍃 The Uluru National Park in the Northern Territory, Australia, bans climbers from Ayers Rock when temperatures reach 38°C. Twenty-four climbers have died of heart failure or heat exhaustion since 1965.

Wednesday September 4

🍃 A special salmon pass is opened on the river Thames at Mapledurham weir in Oxfordshire to help Thames salmon swim up to their spawning grounds in the rivers Lodden, Kennet and Pang.

Thursday September 5

🍃 Pollution levels in cities soar because of the hot, still weather, and triggers rioting and looting in Cardiff, Oxford and Birmingham.

🍃 Two rare soft-plumaged petrels, which rarely stray north of Africa, are 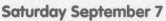 spotted off Flamborough Head, Humberside.

Friday September 6

🍃 Phil Collins, Charlton Heston and Placido Domingo take part in a spectacular concert at Salisbury cathedral in aid of the 123m spire, which is suffering from structural decay. 1,500 lights illuminate the West Front and 2 tonnes of fireworks are let off.

Saturday September 7

🍃 The Batmobile from the Batman TV series is being renovated at Rochdale, Lancs, before going on show at the Cars of the Stars museum in Keswick, Cumbria. It will join Lady Penelope's pink Rolls Royce (FAB 1) from Thunderbirds, Chitty Chitty Bang Bang and several James Bond cars.

Sunday September 8

🍃

🍃 Sir Alec Guinness is awarded the British Film Institute's highest award, the BFI fellowship, to honour his 50yr acting career.

Monday September 9

🍃 Jewish New Year (AM 5752)

🍃 The first edition of *The Big Issue* goes on sale this week. With a print run of 50,000, it is a new monthly magazine, sold by homeless people in aid of the homeless.

Tuesday September 10

🍃 Talks begin in Moscow about the possible sale of the new, unused space station, *Mir 2*, to the United States for $700 million following cuts in the Soviet space programme.

Wednesday September 11

❧ Princess Beatrice (3), daughter of the Duke and Duchess of York spends her first day at nursery school - Upton House School, Windsor.

❧ At the MTV Awards, held this week in Los Angeles, REM wins six awards, including Best Group and Best Video of the Year.

Thursday September 12

❧ US space shuttle, *Discovery*, lifts off from Cape Canaveral, Florida, on a 6-day mission to launch the 6,550kg Upper Atmosphere Research Satellite (UARS) to study changes in the global environment.

Friday September 13

❧ Watch out for Friday the Thirteenth computer virus! Computer buffs put the clocks on their systems forward a day to avoid possible attack.

Saturday September 14

❧ Michelangelo's famous statue of David in the Galleria dell'Academia, Florence, Italy, has its toe damaged by a man with a hammer.

❧ David Hope, former Bishop of Wakefield, is enthroned as Bishop of London in St Paul's Cathedral.

Sunday September 15

❧ Happy 7th birthday to Prince Harry.

❧ Author, Salman Rushdie, who is under a death threat from Iran, comes out of hiding to accept the award for best children's novel from the Writers' Guild for his book *Haroun and the Sea Stories*.

Monday September 16

❧ First class stamps go up by 2p to 24p today and second class stamps go up 1p to 18p.

❧ The all-male Magic Circle, which has 1,400 members all over the world, votes to admit women.

Tuesday September 17

❧ Nobel prize winner, Alexander Solzhenitsyn (72), who was expelled from Russia in 1974, is officially cleared of treason, and can return home after 17yrs exile in the US.

Wednesday September 18

❧ Liverpool FC takes part in its first European competition, after being banned 6yrs ago, beating Kuusyi Lahti, of Finland 6-1 in the UEFA Cup.

❧ An earthquake in Guatemala measures 5.8 on the Richter Scale.

Thursday September 19

❧ Twelve Superdogs are presented with bravery awards by Pedigree Petfoods in Regent's Park, London. They include black labrador Tess, who dragged Arron Whines (2) unconscious from a rock pool when he tripped and fell face down during a seaside trip.

Friday September 20

❧ St James Garlickhythe, in the City of London, a 309-year-old church designed by Sir Christopher Wren, is badly damaged when a crane crashes through the roof.

Saturday September 21

❧ Rock group, Status Quo, celebrates its 25th anniversary by playing in four different arenas in under 12hrs: Sheffield 2pm, Glasgow 4.30pm, Birmingham NEC 7pm and Wembley Arena 9.30pm.

Sunday September 22

🍐 Nigel Matthews (39), of Blythe Bridge, Staffs, wins the title of Britain's Best Milkman.

🍐 A huge 16m tall copy of the Egyptian Sphinx travels across Kowloon harbour to Hong Kong University to promote a production of Verdi's opera *Aida*.

Monday September 23

🍐 The body of a prehistoric 4,000-year-old hunter is discovered in the Similaun Glacier in the Tyrolean Alps. Mummified by the wind, cold and sun and preserved in ice, his bones, teeth, internal organs, skin and fingernails are intact.

Tuesday September 24

🍐 Dr Theodor Seuss Geisel (87), better known as Dr Seuss, the famous American author and illustrator, dies. He taught generations of children that reading could be fun with books like *The Cat in the Hat*, and *Bangers and Mash*.

Wednesday September 25

🍐 A Battle of Britain Spitfire performs a victory roll over RAF Lyneham in Wilts as ex-pilot Jackie Mann (77) arrives home, after being held hostage in Lebanon for 865 days.

Thursday September 26

🍐 Four men and four women are sealed inside the giant Biosphere II greenhouse in the middle of the Arizona desert, at the start of a 2yr experiment to reproduce Earth's ecosystem in a bubble. They will grow their own food and recycle their own waste in seven different climate zones, each with its own plants, animals and insects.

Friday September 27

🍐 Transport Secretary, Malcolm Rifkind, gives the go ahead for the new £75.3 million East London River Crossing at Gallions Reach, Woolwich, which will destroy part of the ancient, 8,000-year-old Oxleas Wood at Greenwich.

Saturday September 28

🍐 Heavy metal group AC/DC stage one of the biggest rock concerts ever in Moscow, in front of an audience of over half a million people.

🍐 Famous American jazz trumpeter, bandleader and composer, Miles Davis (65) dies.

Sunday September 29

🍐 Forbidden Britain Day: The Ramblers' Association organises a nationwide trespass as part of a campaign to open up the countryside to the public and to preserve rights of way. 500 ramblers stride across Thurlstone Moor, S Yorks, one of the most popular sites.

Monday September 30

🍐 Peter Morris (29), of Michigan, USA, scores 371 points to become the first World Scrabble Champion. Lesser-known words on the final Scrabble board include zax (a tool for cutting roof tiles) and ayu (a small Japanese fish).

Tess with Arron

Mysterious Corn Circles

The 1991 Census

April 22 117,000 people begin collecting 23 million Census forms sent to every house in the land by the Office of Population Censuses and Surveys.

Superdog Tess
September 19

Tess the black labrador, is one of 12 superdogs honoured with an award for intelligence and courage.

She was walking with her owner on Swansea beach when she found Arron (2) face down in a rock pool. Tess dragged the unconscious boy to safety before her owner realised what had happened.

January 15 Richard Branson, with his companion Per Lindstrand, lifts off from Japan, landing in the NW Territories of Canada on **January 17** completing the first hot-air balloon crossing of the Pacific.

Richard Branson crossing the Pacific in a balloon

Desert Orchid

Giant Panda Ming Ming

Desert Orchid
December 26

Britain's favourite racehorse, Desert Orchid, retires from racing. In a legendary career he won more than 30 National Hunt races including the King George VI four times, as well as the Cheltenham Gold Cup, the Irish Grand National and the Whitbread Gold Cup.

OCTOBER

Giant Panda Ming Ming arrives at London Zoo

Filmstar Elizabeth Taylor gets married for the 8th time

Tuesday October 1

❖ The Parthenon in Athens is blanketed in haze as smog in the city reaches record levels, despite a government ban on cars.

❖ Thirteen pilot whales stranded on a beach at Cape Cod, Mass, are refloated and swim back out to sea.

Wednesday October 2

❖ Four medals belonging to Capt Philip Durham, of Largo, Fife, who commanded *HMS Defiance* at the Battle of Trafalgar in 1805 and was wounded in the leg and side, are sold for £33,000 at a sale at Phillips, Edinburgh.

Thursday October 3

❖ Britain's longest-running pop show Top of the Pops, which started 28yrs ago, is revamped. It moves to new purpose-built studios at Elstree with a new signature tune and more live music.

Friday October 4

❖ More than 100 of the Queen's swans suffering from a mystery illness, are collected by motor launch on the river Thames nr Windsor, and taken to the Swan Sanctuary nr Egham.

Saturday October 5

❖ From today hugging, kissing and holding hands is banned at Peking University in China. Also unauthorised gatherings, booing and whistling!

Sunday October 6

❖ Western Samoa defeats Wales 16-13 at Cardiff Arms Park in the Rugby World Cup.

❖ A parachutist with a video camera on his helmet lands in the middle of Elizabeth Taylor's wedding to Larry Fortensky (39), at Michael Jackson's Neverland Valley estate in California.

Monday October 7

❖

❖ Data from the Total Ozone Mapping Spectrometer (TOMS) on board the US *Nimbus-7* weather satellite shows that deep holes have appeared in the ozone layer above Antarctica during the southern hemisphere's spring.

Tuesday October 8

❖ Durham Castle, a World Heritage Site, launches a £2.5 million appeal for urgent repairs and restoration.

Wednesday October 9

❖ 1,760 huge yellow umbrellas, nearly 6m high, are unfurled across 29km of Californian countryside. It is the latest piece of modern, outdoor art by Christo, who yesterday unveiled 1,340 blue umbrellas in Japan.

Thursday October 10

❖ Austrian archaeologists, working on the glacier where the body of a prehistoric hunter was found last month, return to Innsbruck with pieces of his trousers, his leather jacket, part of his fur hood and the remains of the animal he caught.

Friday October 11

❖ Ruchi (2½) the Indian lion, has an infected tooth pulled out by the dentist at London Zoo.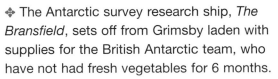

❖ The Antarctic survey research ship, *The Bransfield*, sets off from Grimsby laden with supplies for the British Antarctic team, who have not had fresh vegetables for 6 months.

Saturday October 12

❖ Sleeping Beauty's Castle (Le Chateau de la Belle au Bois Dormant) is unveiled this weekend at Euro Disney, which will open nr Paris, next spring.

Sunday October 13

❖ Chia Chia (Most Wonderful), London Zoo's Giant Panda (19), dies of old age in Chapultepec Zoo, Mexico City, where he has been on loan since 1988. He leaves two offspring - Xin Xin in Mexico and Chu Lin in Madrid.

Monday October 14

❖ Aung San Suu Kyi, the Burmese opposition leader who has been under house arrest for more than 2yrs, is awarded the Nobel Peace Prize for her non-violent struggle against a brutal military dictatorship.

❖ Vivienne Westwood is named British Designer of the Year.

Tuesday October 15

❖ Catamaran passenger ferry *Hoverspeed France* sets a new record for crossing the Channel from Dover to Calais with a time of 34mins 23secs, averaging more than 72kph.

Wednesday October 16

❖ In an auction of 16 ITV licences, Thames TV in London, breakfast channel TV-am, TVS in the South and TSW in the South-West lose their franchises from Jan. 1993 to newcomers Carlton TV, Sunrise, Meridien Broadcasting and Westcountry TV.

Thursday October 17

❖ Gales batter the north of England and Scotland - a 160kph gust is recorded in the Cairngorms.

❖ The Princess of Wales opens the £100 million exhibition hall, Earls Court 2, the biggest new building of its kind in London for 46yrs.

Friday October 18

❖ The first snow of the English winter falls at Great Longstone, Derbys.

❖ Storms sweep the North Sea as 200 men are airlifted to safety from oil rigs between Shetland and Aberdeen.

Saturday October 19

❖ Ming Ming (Brilliance), a female Giant Panda (11), arrives at London Zoo from China. She settles in well after her flight from Hong Kong and tucks into a large meal of bamboo shoots.

Sunday October 20

❖ Brazilian racing driver, Ayrton Senna, wins his third World Championship, coming second in the Japanese Grand Prix.

❖ A powerful earthquake devastates the foothills of the Himalayas in northern India. It measures 6.1 on the Richter Scale and kills more than 1,600 people.

Monday October 21

❖ Apple Day.

❖ A joint British-Australian team lifts off from Gokyo, in Nepal, and makes the first-ever flight over 8,848m Mount Everest by hot-air balloon, landing 45mins later in Tibet.

Tuesday October 22

❖ Michelangelo's famous statue of David in the Galleria dell'Academia, Florence, which was attacked last month by a man with a hammer, has had its toe glued back on.

❖ Ben Okri wins the Booker Prize in London for his novel *The Famished Road* about a Nigerian spirit child.

Wednesday October 23

❖

❖ Prince William (9) and Prince Harry (7) start their first official foreign visit, a 7 day tour of Canada, with their parents, the Prince and Princess of Wales.

Thursday October 24

❖ Emperor Akihito of Japan presents his first grandchild, a baby girl who was born last night, with a traditional sword for self-protection. She is called Mako and weighs 3.2 kg.

Friday October 25

❖ Trekkies gather at the Star Trek Official Fan Club in Aurora, Colorado, USA, to mourn Gene Roddenberry, (70) who died yesterday. He created the original television series with the Star Ship Enterprise, Captain Kirk and Dr Spock.

Saturday October 26

❖ Dominic O'Brien (34), operations manager at Stansted Airport, wins the first World Memory Championships at the Atheneum, London. He sets a new world record for memorising the order of a pack of cards in 2mins 29secs.

Sunday October 27

❖ British Summer Time ends at 2am when clocks go back 1hr.

❖ Canadian singer, Bryan Adams, loses his place at No.1 in the charts after a record sixteen weeks at the top with *Everything I do, I do it for you*. He is toppled by U2 with *The Fly*.

Monday October 28

❖ At an auction of 452 car number plates in Glasgow, JIMMY is sold for £35,000.

❖ British Rail tries out a new £260,000 train fitted with special rotating brushes to sweep leaves off the tracks.

Tuesday October 29

❖ The US *Galileo* spacecraft, which is on its way to Jupiter, takes the first-ever picture of an asteroid called Gaspra, which orbits between Mars and Jupiter.

Wednesday October 30

❖ The Queen opens the new £86 million Dartford Bridge across the river Thames. Drivers will be able to use a new electronic card to pay the 80p toll, mounted on the windscreen and 'read' by a radio signal.

Thursday October 31

❖ Hallowe'en.

❖ Sindy celebrates her 30th birthday at a nightclub in London, wearing a new pink dress by British Designer of the Year, Vivienne Westwood. 31 million Sindy dolls have been sold since she first appeared in 1961.

Personalities of 1991

Nigel Kennedy
Punk violinist. On **June 20** he is made an Honorary Doctor of Letters at Bath University

Andre Agassi
Trendy tennis player

Sinead O'Connor
Shaven headed pop singer who boycotts awards ceremonies because they are too commercial

Hannibal the Cannibal
Silence of the Lambs

Jason Donovan
Stars in new production of *Joseph and the Amazing Technicolour Dreamcoat*

Helen Sharman
First British astronaut

**John McCarthy
Terry Waite**
Released Beirut hostages

The Big Issue
Launched

Similaun Man
Deep frozen prehistoric hunter found in a glacier on the borders of Austria and Italy

Vivienne Westwood
British designer of the year for the second time

Vivienne Westwood *(left)* with model Holly Wilcox

Nigel Kennedy

Sinead O'Connor

Andre Agassi

Jason Donovan as *Joseph*

Launch of *The Big Issue* – a magazine sold by the homeless for the homeless

Below: Helen Sharman, Britain's first astronaut, with a model of the *Mir* spaceship in which she will make her flight

Above: Pictured at the launch of *The Big Issue* are John Bird (editor), with supporters Shelia McKechnie from Shelter, and Gordon and Anita Roddick of the Body Shop

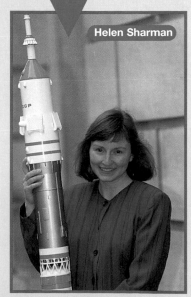
Helen Sharman

✳ NOVEMBER ✳

Last oil well is put out in Kuwait
Sting wins his fight to save the Brazilian rainforest

Friday November 1

✳ North Atlantic storms batter the east coast of the USA. President Bush's holiday home at Kennebunkport, Maine, is badly damaged by 9m waves.

Saturday November 2

✳ Australia wins the final of the rugby World Cup at Twickenham, beating England 12-6.

✳ Hundreds of passengers are stranded as BR's new hi-tech trains are delayed or cancelled because of leaves on the line.

Sunday November 3

✳ Snow in Glos., the Pennines and the Lake District.

✳ Liz McColgan (27), of Scotland, wins the New York marathon at her first attempt in a time of 2hrs 27mins 32secs. The men's race is won by Salvador Garcia, of Mexico, in 2hrs 9mins 28secs.

Monday November 4

✳ Blackpool Pleasure Beach gets planning permission for a giant 72m high rollercoaster that will be more than 1.5km long. The rides will travel at 137kph.

Tuesday November 5

✳ Bonfire Night.

✳ The body of millionaire newspaper tycoon, Robert Maxwell, is found in the Atlantic after he is reported missing from his yacht

The Lady Ghislaine which had been cruising the Canaries.

✳ Tropical storm Thelma hits the central Philippines, causing the worst landslides and floods for years. 5,400 people are killed and 50,000 are left homeless.

Wednesday November 6

✳ Sheikh Jaber Ahmed al-Sabah, emir of Kuwait, formally puts out the last of hundreds of oil wells, which have been blazing since the end of the Gulf War. The retreating Iraqi army set them on fire, causing the worst oilfield disaster ever.

Thursday November 7

✳ Grand Duke Vladimir Kirillovich (74), a cousin of the last Czar Nicholas II and heir to the Russian throne, visits his homeland for the first time and attends the ceremony in which the city of Leningrad is renamed St Petersburg.

Friday November 8

✳ Astronomers from Arizona University at the Kitt Peak Observatory Arizona, USA, have spotted a UFO heading for Earth this week, but they don't know whether it is an asteroid or an old piece of rocket.

Saturday November 9

✳ 150 floats leave Guildhall at the start of the Lord Mayor's Show in London. The new Lord Mayor, Sir Brian Jenkins, chooses 'The City Serving Europe' as the theme.

Sunday November 10
* Remembrance Sunday.

* 5,200 tonne Swedish freighter, *SK Link One,* carrying 8,000 tonnes of timber and wood, blows up and sinks off the coast of Cleveland, when a fire starts in the engine room. It leaves a 1.5km oil slick.

Monday November 11
* Author, Salman Rushdie, spends his 1,000th day in hiding under the death sentence (fatwa) issued by the late Ayatollah Khomeini. It was pronounced on February 14, 1989, after the publication of his book *The Satanic Verses*.

Tuesday November 12
* Violent gales and electrical storms sweep Wales and the West Country.

* US beachcombers scour beaches in Oregon, trying to pair up thousands of Nike trainers. They were packed in 5 large containers which were washed overboard from a cargo ship in the Pacific last year.

Wednesday November 13
* A tornado tears through the village of Dullingham, Cambs, tearing down buildings and power lines.

* French actor and singer, Yves Montand, who died on Saturday, is buried at Père Lachaise Cemetery in Paris. Mourners include Gerard Depardieu, Alain Delon and Catherine Deneuve.

Thursday November 14
* Michael Jackson's new £35 million video, *Black or White*, gets its first British screening on 'Top of the Pops' tonight. Directed by John Landis, it co-stars Macaulay Culkin and Bart Simpson.

Friday November 15
* Winston Churchill's grey homburg hat, with gold initials WSC, is sold at a Christie's auction in London for £7,260.

Saturday November 16
* 5,226 competitors take part in the World Budgerigar Championships in Doncaster. A grey green bird, belonging to AV Smith, of Sheffield, wins the Best in Show title.

Sunday November 17
* Twitchers flock to Stone Creek, nr Hull, on the Humber Estuary, to see a tiny bird called a Mugimaki flycatcher. It has been blown thousands of km off course while migrating from its breeding grounds in Asia.

Monday November 18
* Terry Waite, the former Church of England special envoy, is freed after being held hostage by Islamic Jihad in Beirut for 1,763 days. Released with him is American, Dr Thomas Sutherland, who was held for 2,353 days.

Tuesday November 19
* Rolling Stones, Mick Jagger (48), Keith Richards (47) and Ronnie Wood (44), sign a £30 million three-album deal with Virgin Records. The band, which also includes Charlie Watts and Bill Wyman, was launched in 1962 and has had 37 top singles.

Wednesday November 20
* *Dangerous*, Michael Jackson's first new album for 4yrs, is launched at the Savoy Hotel, London. *Thriller*, released in 1982, sold 45 million copies and is still the best-selling album ever.

Thursday November 21

* Frenchman, Gerard d'Aboville, lands at Ilwaco, Washington State, USA, after rowing single-handed across the Pacific. It took him 133 days to complete the 10,056km journey, from Choshi in Japan.

Friday November 22

* A T-shirt belonging to Mick Jagger fetches £200, and a guitar signed by members of Genesis is sold for £850 at a celebrity auction in London in aid of Shelter's new £3 million appeal.

Saturday November 23

* A 1904 6d lilac-brown IR Official stamp, featuring the profile of Edward VII, is sold for a record £33,000 at Sotheby's, London this week, setting a new record for a single 20th century British stamp.

Sunday November 24

* The 2,253km four-day Lombard RAC Rally starts in Harrogate.

* Graham Kentfield, becomes new Chief Cashier at the Bank of England this week. His signature will appear on all new banknotes.

Monday November 25

* Agatha Christie's play *The Mousetrap* celebrates its 40th birthday in the West End. Opening in 1952, with Richard Attenborough and Sheila Sim in the leading roles, it is the longest-running theatre production of any kind.

Tuesday November 26

* An exhibition of water-colours and lithographs by the Prince of Wales opens at the Norton Gallery in West Palm Beach, California, USA.

* US space shuttle, *Atlantis*, passes within 40km of the Soviet space station, *Mir*. The crews say hallo via radio.

Wednesday November 27

* Rock star Sting succeeds in his campaign to save the homeland of 2,000 Kayapo Indians in the Brazilian rainforest when President Fernando Collor de Mello agrees to give it protected status. The new park covers 181,300 sq km around the river Xingu.

Thursday November 28

* US Thanksgiving Day.

* Six astronauts celebrate Thanksgiving at 29,000kph on board US space shuttle, *Atlantis*, and eat a traditional dinner of rehydrated turkey.

Friday November 29

* Sir Clive Sinclair announces his latest invention - a new electric bicycle that will be powered by a combination of batteries and pedalling.

Saturday November 30

* National Tree Dressing Day.

* The USA wins the first World Soccer championship for women with a 2-1 victory over Norway in Guangzhou, China.

STAMPS OF THE YEAR 1991

❄ FEBRUARY 5 ❄
PO issued a Greetings Booklet
of Stamps called *Good Luck*

❄ MARCH 5 ❄
PO issued four new stamps to
mark scientific achievements

❖ APRIL 23 ❖
PO issued a new set of stamps
entitled Europa - Europe in Space

❄ JANUARY 8 ❄
PO issued five new
stamps of dog paintings
by George Stubbs

❀ JUNE 11 ❀
PO issued four
new stamps to
celebrate the
World Student
Games

☀ AUGUST 20 ☀
PO issued five new stamps to mark the 150th
Anniversary of Dinosaur Identification by Owen

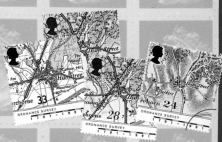

NOVEMBER 12
PO issued five Christmas stamps - illuminated
manuscripts from the Bodleian Library

SEPTEMBER 17
PO issued four new stamps
to celebrate the bicentenary
of Ordinance Survey

✳ DECEMBER ✳

1991 Year of the Maze

Sunday December 1
✳ World Aids Day.

✳ US space shuttle, *Atlantis*, lands at Edwards Air Force Base, California, 3 days early because of a fault in the navigation unit.

✳ The French tennis team, captained by Yannick Noah, wins the Davis Cup for the first time in 59yrs.

Monday December 2
✳ His Holiness the Dalai Lama, Tibet's exiled spiritual leader, visits Prime Minister, John Major, at No. 10 Downing Street for just under an hour.

Tuesday December 3
✳ A Dinky model of a Heinz Tomato ketchup lorry, bought in 1959 for the equivalent of 45p, is sold for £1,600 at an auction at Sherborne, Dorset.

✳ Marco Pierre White (29), who runs Harveys restaurant in Wandsworth, wins the Chef of the Year award in London.

Wednesday December 4
✳ Terry Anderson, the last US hostage in Lebanon, is released after nearly 7yrs in captivity, and meets his daughter, Sulome (6), whom he has never seen before.

Thursday December 5
✳ A special concert is held in St Paul's Cathedral, London, to commemorate the 200th anniversary of Mozart's death. His Requiem is performed by the London Mozart Players, beginning at midnight and ending at 1am, the time of his death in 1791.

Friday December 6
✳

✳ The acre is to be officially replaced by the hectare at the end of 1994, under a European Community directive.

✳ A manuscript of Beethoven's Piano Sonata in E Minor, Opus 90, dated August 16, 1814, is sold at Sotheby's, London, for a record £1.1 million.

Saturday December 7
✳ 88 people are injured when the 7am Portsmouth to Cardiff train crashes into the back of the 8.30am London to Cardiff Inter-City express in the Severn Tunnel.

✳ President Bush attends a special ceremony in Pearl Harbour to mark the 50th anniversary of the bombing of the American fleet by Japanese warplanes that brought the US into World War II.

Sunday December 8
✳ Steven Spielberg's latest film *Hook*, an updated version of J M Barrie's famous children's story *Peter Pan*, is premiered in Los Angeles. It stars Dustin Hoffman and Robin Williams, with Julia Roberts as Tinkerbelle.

Monday December 9
✳ Leaders of the twelve EEC nations meet in Maastricht, Holland, at the start of a historic summit to decide on political and monetary union.

Tuesday December 10

✳ Europe's first factory for recycling tyres into rubber granules to make safety surfaces for children's playgrounds opens at Newark, Notts.

Wednesday December 11

✳ -13°C in Surrey, the coldest day of the year so far.

✳ Two pieces of the Berlin Wall are given to the Prince of Wales, as Christmas presents for Prince William and Prince Harry.

Thursday December 12

✳ Middlesbrough is named Environment City of the Year by the Royal Society for Nature Conservation.

✳ The 2p toll for pedestrians over the Clifton suspension bridge in Bristol is scrapped after 127yrs.

Friday December 13

✳ Best night of the year for seeing the famous Geminid meteor shower!

✳ Titian's 'Venus and Adonis', painted in 1555, is sold for a world record price of £7,480,000 at Christie's, London.

Saturday December 14

✳ The Olympic Flame, lit yesterday by the sun's rays at the Temple of Hera, Greece, travels by Concorde to Paris, on the first leg of its journey to next year's Winter Games in Albertville.

Sunday December 15

✳ Liz McColgan (27), Scotland's world 10,000m gold medallist, is named BBC Sports Personality of the Year.

✳ Queen's *Bohemian Rhapsody*, re-released after the death of lead singer Freddie Mercury, zooms to No. 1 in the charts. It was originally top of the pops in 1975.

Monday December 16

✳ All main stations in London are closed for several hours today after an IRA bomb explodes on the railway line outside Clapham Junction.

✳ Stella Rimington is appointed the first female head of MI5, Britain's secret service.

Tuesday December 17

✳ A fire guts the Fun House on Blackpool Pleasure Beach, destroying the Wall of Death, early dodgem cars and antique waltzers. The head of the famous Laughing Man survives because it had been removed for a face lift.

Wednesday December 18

✳ At a Sotheby's sale in New York, a wedding dress worn by Madonna is sold for £6,000, a 1955 guitar that belonged to the late Jimi Hendrix fetches £11,000, and Bill Haley's first electric guitar goes for £15,200.

Thursday December 19

✳ Britain is hit by the worst winds of winter. Gusts of 177kph are recorded in the Western Isles.

✳ A white rhinestone glove, worn by Michael Jackson in the video for *Thriller,* is bought by the Hard Rock Cafe in Piccadilly for £16,500 at Christie's, London.

Friday December 20

✳ Heavy snow in Scotland, N. Ireland and the north of England.

✳ A fossilised nautiloid, a squid-like creature that lived 95 million years ago, goes on show at the Natural History Museum, London. It was found earlier in the year by Channel Tunnel diggers.

Saturday December 21

* Partial eclipse of the Moon.

* Goodbye to the USSR as leaders of eleven former Soviet republics formally sign a declaration founding a new looser union, the Commonwealth of Independent States.

Sunday December 22

* Shortest day.

* An RAF helicopter takes emergency supplies, including turkeys, Christmas trees and Christmas post, to 17 people stranded on Lundy Island for more than a week, after storms in the Bristol Channel.

Monday December 23

* Gales sweep the country with a gust of 156kph recorded at the Mumbles, nr Swansea. The public lobby in the Houses of Parliament is out of bounds because of the danger of falling masonry.

Tuesday December 24

* Christmas Eve.

* Top selling present this year is Nintendo's Game Boy (£70), including a game called Tetris. It contains an 8-bit processor. More than 10 million have been sold worldwide.

Wednesday December 25

* Christmas Day.

* In her traditional Christmas Day speech, the Queen announces that she is not proposing to abdicate in favour of Prince Charles.

* The *Mir* cosmonauts broadcast a special message from more than 240 km above Earth encouraging people all over the world to use science wisely.

Thursday December 26

* Boxing Day.

* The famous grey steeplechaser, *Desert Orchid*, falls at the third last fence while trying to win the King George VI Rank Chase at Kempton Park for a record fifth time, and goes into retirement.

Friday December 27

* Hungarian chess player, Judit Polgar (15yrs 5months), becomes the youngest-ever Grandmaster by winning the National Championship in Budapest, Hungary. She breaks the record held by Bobby Fischer for more than 33yrs.

Saturday December 28

* After 40yrs in London, the Miss World contest is held in Atlanta, Georgia, USA. Miss Venezuela, Ninibeth Beatriz Leal Jimenez (20), wins the crown, with Miss Australia, Leanne Buckle (21), the runner-up.

Sunday December 29

* The *Aileach*, a 12m square-rigged Hebridean galley rows up the Thames to the London International Boat Show. Built by the Lords of the Isles Galley Trust, it is modelled on boats used by the Scots and Irish in the 15th century.

Monday December 30

* Italian tenor, Luciano Pavarotti, gives a special concert in Dublin to mark the end of the Irish capital's term as the European Community's City of Culture.

Tuesday December 31

* In the New Year's Honours List, published today; actor George Cole is made an OBE and Sir Brian Rix becomes Lord Rix of Whitehall, for his work as chairman of Mencap.

* The twelve huge bells of St Paul's Cathedral, each weighing 13.5 tonnes, ring out the old year for the first time in 46yrs.